May

Julie Murray

Abdo
MONTHS
Kids

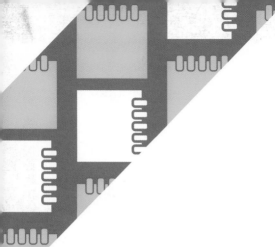

abdopublishing.com

Published by Abdo Kids, a division of ABDO, PO Box 398166, Minneapolis, Minnesota 55439.
Copyright © 2018 by Abdo Consulting Group, Inc. International copyrights reserved in all countries.
No part of this book may be reproduced in any form without written permission from the publisher.

Printed in the United States of America, North Mankato, Minnesota.

052017

092017

 THIS BOOK CONTAINS
RECYCLED MATERIALS

Photo Credits: iStock, Shutterstock, ©dbking p.9 / CC-BY 2.0

Production Contributors: Teddy Borth, Jennie Forsberg, Grace Hansen

Design Contributors: Christina Doffing, Candice Keimig, Dorothy Toth

Publisher's Cataloging in Publication Data

Names: Murray, Julie, 1969-, author.

Title: May / by Julie Murray.

Description: Minneapolis, Minnesota : Abdo Kids, 2018 | Series: Months |
    Includes bibliographical references and index.

Identifiers: LCCN 2016962337 | ISBN 9781532100192 (lib. bdg.) |
    ISBN 9781532100888 (ebook) | ISBN 9781532101434 (Read-to-me ebook)

Subjects: LCSH: May (Month)--Juvenile literature. | Calendar--Juvenile literature.

Classification: DDC 398/.33--dc23

LC record available at http://lccn.loc.gov/2016962337

Table of Contents

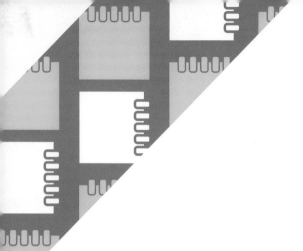

May

There are 12 months
in the year.

January

February

March

April

May

June

July

August

September

October

November

December

5

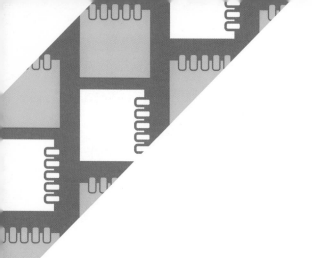

May is the 5th month.

It has 31 days.

May

1	2	3	4	5	6	7
8	9	10	11	12	13	14
15	16	17	18	19	20	21
22	23	24	25	26	27	28
29	30	31				

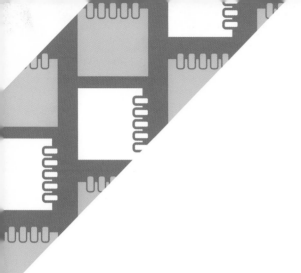

Celebrate **Cinco de Mayo**.

It is on the 5th.

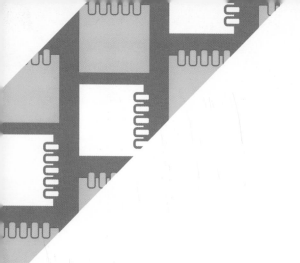

Iris hugs her mom. It's Mother's Day! It is the 2nd Sunday.

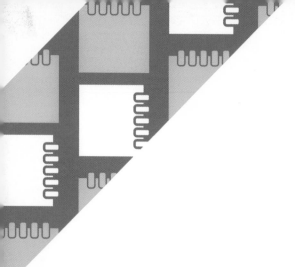

Memorial Day is in May.

It is the last Monday.

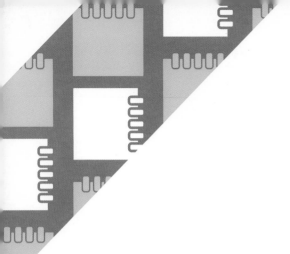

The air is warm. Flowers **bloom**.

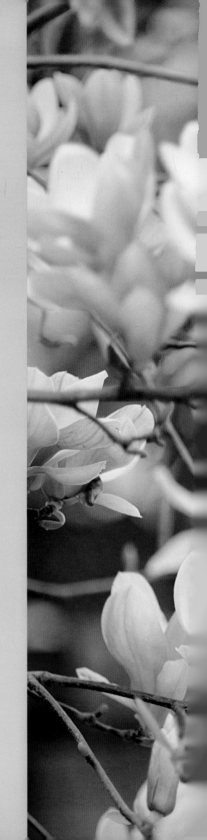

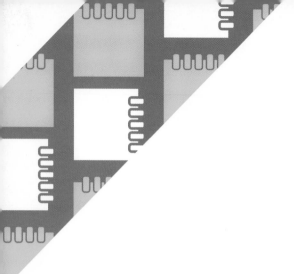

Alex plays soccer.

He scores a goal!

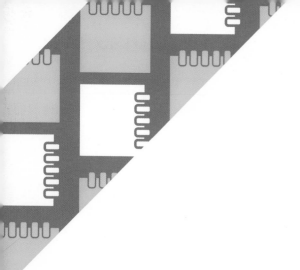

Kate walks her dog.

They enjoy the park.

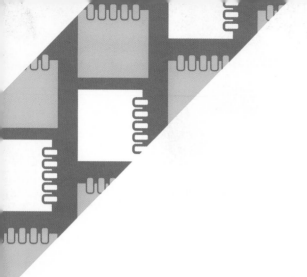

Hugo rides his bike.

He loves May!

Fun Days in May

Star Wars Day
May 4

National Maritime Day
May 22

National Tap Dance Day
May 25

National Paper Airplane Day
May 26

Glossary

bloom
produce flowers.

Cinco de Mayo
Spanish for "Fifth of May," a day that celebrates Mexican culture and heritage.

Memorial Day
a holiday in the United States that remembers those who died while serving in the armed forces.

Index

abdokids.com

Use this code to log on to abdokids.com and access crafts, games, videos, and more!

Abdo Kids Code:
MMK0192